NEAR WHERE THE BLOOD POOLS

A NOVEL IN VERSE

BEN TERRY

LIVINGSTON PRESS
UNIVERSITY OF WEST ALABAMA

Library of Congress Control Number 2024935495

Printed on acid-free paper
Printed in the United States of America by
Publishers Graphics

Typesetting and page layout: Eleanor Boudreau, Joe Taylor,
Proofreading: Tricia Taylor, Summer Chadwick,
Annsley Johnsey, Savannah Beams, Brooke Barger, Kelly West

SPECIAL THANKS TO ELEANOR BOUDREAU FOR HER WORK ON THIS BOOK.

Cover Design: Ben Shadden

6 5 4 3 2 1

NEAR WHERE THE BLOOD POOLS

Near Where the Blood Pools
Contents

Winter

Character List

(in order of appearance)

Hope Purdy – Cephas' little sister

Memphis Sumtner – Marl Mae's daddy *(Seer)*

Jon Marc – Cephas' best friend

Marl Mae Glee Purdy – Cephas' mother

Cephas Purdy – main character

Fortner Yeoman Purdy – Cephas' father

Lou Ellen – Jon Marc's sister and Cephas' paramour

Church ladies

Joela Cozak – Cephas' heartbreak revelation

The Quaker – Joela's parrot

Hill Bros. tin of ashes

Maude – Jon Marc and Lou Ellen's mother

Dilly – Lou Ellen's father

Gentry and Lomax – treasure hunters

Toot Van Oster – Rummy's great-great-grandmother

Rummy Van Oster – pig farmer

Milo Bittle – town drunk

Ham-fisted Charlie – Neon Sign bartender

Hoot – Marl's new asylum friend

Reverend Good – Preacher from Marl's youth

Sheriff –

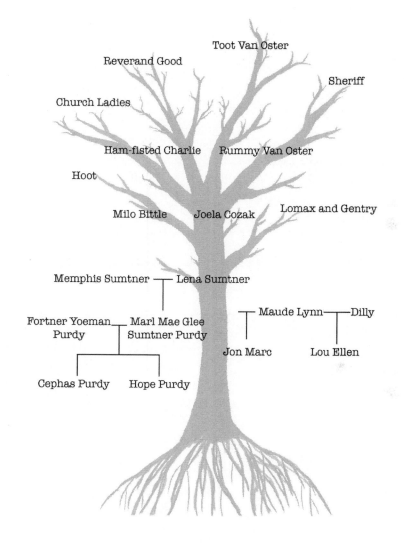

Author's Note

While I desired to tell a story about a specific family, I also wanted to explore the themes of loss, the unexpected brutality of life, and the tenuous distance between this existence and the next.

I've tried to craft each piece in such a way it is capable of standing on its own. Some I succeeded with, others not so much. In the end, the greater goal was to share a story with enough levels of character development and story depth to appeal to a much wider readership than just "poetry people."

The fluid nature of time being one of the major themes, the reader is sometime taken in and out of the present to visit events elsewhere. Because this is essentially the telling of an 80,000 word story in about 12,000 words, the disappearance of Hope, in her eleventh year, serves as the epochal event all other time is anchored from.

Hope Exists — Losing Hope — Hope Gone — What Remains

Of course there's a lot of metaphor and some deeply woven threads for the lit nerds out there, but on the surface, if you just read it as you would any old novel (hopefully) you'll find intriguing and relatable characters, a suggestive "whodunit?" plot line, and all the best earmarks of a great big Southern Gothic novel.

I'm not certain I accomplished everything I initially set out to do, but best case scenario, I didn't get in the way of this story ending up the best version of what it could be.

—Cheers

Ben Terry

…give unto them beauty for ashes,

the oil of joy for mourning,

the garment of praise

for the spirit of heaviness…

—KJV Isaiah 61:3

LOSING HOPE
The Year

The Search for Marl Mae's Hope

A clue is found — summer

The wild swing of light and shadow
puppets cast among the ivy and brambles
animate the woods behind the Purdy home.

Shouts echoing off each other
fall whimpering to the ground
as weak-willed bottle rockets
on a muggy, windless night.

All gives way to dawn.

Called in by Memphis,
Jon Marc and Marl Mae
sit around the kitchen table,
torn and ragged as the night.
Licking her thumb, Marl reaches
for a puckered tear of blood.
Briar scratch beneath Jon Marc's eye.
Old and dry, wets her thumb a second time
to cull the sanguine dust from his face.
"Cephas, even your dirt and blood taste stubborn."
He finds a smile for Marl that
hangs sad across his boyish face.

The screen door groans and claps.
Fortner trudges into the kitchen,
trading his flashlight for a cup of coffee

in the weathered hand of Memphis.

Weariness knew no better home
than the features of Fortner Yeoman Purdy.

Ruby red, the morning sky
throws a sailor's warning through the window.
Storm clouds gathering atop the mountains.

"She fell in a mine or else
got lost along the river. Otherwise
that shittin'-ass dog would've surely turned up."

Marl rose with fire in her fists and eyes for Fortner.
Brought still by her father's
outstretched arm between them.
Following its length with her gaze,
the gnarled finger took her
East, out the window

to Lou Ellen, statuesque in the yard,
holding fast the streamered handlebars of their child's bike.

Marl Mae boils to a scalding swell,
pouring forth in a keening wail.
Collapsed with forearms against
Fortner, she gnashes her teeth at his chest
as the first clap of thunder
bears forth the late summer rain,
and blood stains her chin
beneath the torn shirt and
flesh at her mouth.

We Come to Pray with You

Ladies from church try to condole Marl Mae — fall

"When will you be expecting
to hold the service?"

This ain't the Bible.
Lost don't mean dead.

"You must grieve some.
Ain't healthy not to."

I'm grieving alright,
over answering the door.

"Don't be nasty. We don't
mean to bother."

But you do, and
do, and do it well.

"Tell that, Marl Mae,
to the Father. Confess yourself."

What's to say?
I love my child.

"Surely you've some sin.
Lighten your burden, take up the Lord's."

Ya'll come to pray for me,

is that it?

"We come to bear with you, Sister,
to feed you'uns with love and covered dish."

Well, Lord knows
I need your casseroles,

condemnation, and asses
wearing out my couch

like a thread-worn brothel
needs a bag of broken dicks.

Gossip flurries like flies on shit.
Everyone eager to get their fill.

"Ladies, I don't believe
Marl Mae is well."

HOPE EXISTS
7 Years Before

Cephas Touches Death in Childhood

Cephas, age 9, and Marl Mae take a trip to the river — fall

Marl Mae, she dips her toes into the creek,
"See, sweet Cephas, it's like time travel
cause the water you step in
ain't the same as where you're standing now.
Everything flowing by, done happened
somewhere up stream
somewhere before.
Same as us right here
right now,
and the water carries it all
down like a leaf.

"It ain't like the wind.

"You can't see yourself in the wind.
Not like the water, pulling
and tugging and pulling,
whipping away little pieces
of you.
Time travel makes things
blurry around the edges
cause it ain't here
and it ain't then.
And if you ain't standing
careful still
you won't recognize yourself.

"See now, hush, baby Cephas,
while Mama holds you down.
You got the eyes for seeing
like your Grandpap.
I heard it in a dream.
Tell Mama what you see."

The cold chilled him something fierce.
Hard, tried to see through the dirty current,
to see for his mama.
To see like Memphis.
The water carried his daddy's voice.
He could hear it now,
just as his lungs burned
and his legs started kicking.
He tried not to move.
He had to hold still for Mama.
Nothin' felt better than Mama's…

The dark crowded his eyes now.
Too soon, too soon.
He hadn't seen nothing yet.

With a deep, deep breath
he swallowed time,
and it burned like fire in his chest,
smelled of stone and sand and decay.

Then the light came,
and he retched up time
and creek and visions

and everything he'd seen
rolling by.

And there sat his daddy
heaving wind and curses.
Mud-sopped and hair plastered
to his skull.
Ribbons of red
lacing through the watercress,
and Marl Mae, smiling stone still,
on her side with her toes in the creek.
He could tell he done good.
Marl Mae was smiling,
but smiling queer.

LOSING HOPE
The Year

Searching the Past

Cephas, age 16, returns to the river alone — summer

Closing his eyes to remember,
feels the shifting earth press against his palms,
push the skin back at his cuticles
as he digs his fingers in,
bracing against the sodden bank,
stares hard at the version of himself
gazing back from time since carried away,
wonders at the past and future
well evolved into sediment and refuse
too fine to know with naked eyes.

Breathe, Cephas, breathe deeply.
Take in all your breathe,
every sip of this moment,
he remembers her say,
"How you'll find your way
back from where you'll go, from what you'll see
is the air you now breathe.
When you have nothing left
it will be what you're seeking
has room to find you."

And he wonders,
does his best to recall
a glimpse of Hope.
Anything.
A deflated nothing.

Shame fills him
as the cowardice leaches
from his eyes,
drips from his cheeks,
to be carried away with time and memories
he cannot bring himself to recall,
histories he cannot bring himself to fetch.
Not since he first touched death.

WHAT REMAINS
Year 4

The Highway

Cephas, age 21, picks up a hitchhiker — fall

Mindless concrete running away
until it's no place to go.

Nothing good ever came from
the absence of dirt and gravel.
Why's everything got to be so goddamn gray?
Evergreen, hell!

Scotch pine and hemlocks
walking up hill
both sides of the road.

Yellow – yellow – yellow.
Truck tires lick up the stripes
as he crowds the centerline,
passing them out the back
like tapeworms from a metal dog.

Laughing he remembers
his sister's bitch cur,
Freckles.

"Eat and shit, eat and shit.
All the goddamn dog does
is eat and shit,"
his daddy would cuss.

Faded hatchback
huddled on the shoulder
like a sorry Easter egg.
Rust creeping up the fender wells,
peeking through the bumper.

Black plastic trash bag
half stretched over the door frame,
slouches like a limp dick
waving "hi" as he blows by.

Plastic sack of hamburgers
disappeared off the neighbor's grill.

They raised hell with Fortner.
Swore us wormy-ass kids took it.

Daddy hit the son of a bitch so hard
a three-day punch grew into two weeks
in the county jail.

Sent him tumbling backwards over his own grill.
An ashy gray coal
bucked up skyward,
field goaled those big ol' titties—
neighbor's yuck-mouthed wife
squealed like Satan was
carving his name on her.

Bologna tits, they called her,
after a drunken 4th.

Yuck-mouth flipped her mams out,
a regular trailer park fireworks show.

Twelve days short of daddy coming home,
a yellow grocery sack comes hanging
half out of Freckles' pucker-knot
like a tapeworm.
Set his sister to crying.

Blue jean jacket and black dress,
flash of white goose flesh,
wind whipping the hem above her knees
stride for stride.

Wherever she's headed
it's on purpose.
Curled in on herself,
like she's guarding a candle flame.

Five miles from nothing
his mind stutters a moment;
some dope whore
running from her man.

Goddamn, he swears beneath his breath.
Too late now cause
he's already slowing down.

She don't run,
just keeps striding.
Hair lapping her face,

inch high, she grows beautiful
in the rearview.

Elbowing the door,
she stands there like a penitent,
head down in the cold.

"Handle works!" he yells.
She knocks again.

Cussing himself swell,
We got a live one here folks,
leans over to open the door.
Dress slides to her thigh.
With a foot in the cab,
she uses her knocking elbow
to heft herself in.

Reaches out to pull it to.

She's got hands after all.
The truck's tires buzz across
the drunk line marking the shoulder.

He flips the heater on as an afterthought.
Watches a bit of leaf sputter up from the vent,
flutter down to the seat between them,
landing on the mountaintop of my Hills Bros.' rusted lid.

Slowly she unfolds,
revealing a little green bird

cupped, shivering,
against her chest.

"Quaker," she says.

"I'll say, and colder than
picnic chicken."

"A parrot."

"Yeah, that too."
He smiles at his joke.

She ain't just rearview beautiful,
she's real beautiful.
Reaching forward,
he cranks the heater.

Jon Marc and the Neon Sign

Jon Marc and Cephas, age 21, meet for a drink — winter

"Cephas Purdy, you're the shit stain runt
of a broken volcano and a wild paint,
and nary a hair resides upon your sorry hide
if this bourbon at elbow left
ain't the first to punch your dance card."

"Well-read, you might be. A poet you ain't, Jon Marc.
As for insults, I'm cut deepest
by your lack of recollection,
not six years gone, you bloodied my nose
over the sight of my hairy ass
giving Lou Ellen a poke
in the back of your mama's Chevy."

"Like the scrolls of Babylon's forbidden religions
there are things never to be discussed.
My sister's charitable nature being foremost.
Now drink aforementioned whiskey and entertain me
before I dot your eye in ode to spiritual enlightenment."

Cephas gently sets my Hill Bros.' tin
on the stained formica tabletop.
Licking the split knuckle of this thumb
he brings the bourbon to his mouth
and lets the meanness of it bloom
a cinder against his wind-chapped lips
as Grandpap spoke again to his ear,

"It's a sad evil for a man to
rush through pain like it were a blemished offering
from the Maker."

He tilts the shot back in prayer,
and sucks his teeth,
as Jon Marc racks a diamond of nine,
chalks his finger like a cue
and dots the waitress' nose
before rolling back in retreat,
pleading mercy and another round.

Cephas, laying a steady hand on my rusted lid,
rises to bring chaos, then geometry
to the tired felt while his friend
patiently waits.

HOPE GONE
Year 2

Cephas Talks with Maude

Cephas, age 17 — fall

"Cephas, why do you hate women so much?"

"I don't hate 'em,
I love 'em."

"Yeah, well darling, you
can poke 'em and
still hate 'em,
and hate 'em you do."

"Ain't no one said anything about poking."

"No one ain't got to
when I can smell it in my Chevy
as sure as a Christmas ham.
And if that ain't enough,
I ain't seen Jon Marc
with busted knuckles since
Dilly skinned out."

Baboon-ass red, Cephas turned
under the naked 40 watt
dangling dead center of the kitchen
like a lonely hangman's noose.

Maude was too beautiful
to be someone's mama,

Cephas had always believed.
But the pencil-fine, pink scar
running from her left ear
down her neck until
it got lost somewhere
in her cleavage
said she was capable of anything.

"Ain't no sense in getting blushed up
about it now."

Sudden aware he'd been looking
Jon Marc's mama in the chest,
Cephas caught her eye, but
she made no mind of it,
swatting his shoulder
with her dish towel like always.

"Lou Ellen knows what she's doing.
She's a smart one,
but hornier than a tomcat.
Jon Marc's got the Army and his college.
It's you that worries me."

Cephas rocked back on the dinette chair,
studied the tin lid of the Hills Bros.' can,
running a finger along its edge
like the imaginary scar
he'd traced
from Lou Ellen's left ear,
down her neck until

it came to the last button
left on her shirt.

"Some might think it's strange,
you carrying Memphis around
like you do."

Pausing, he stared hard through the can
until a rumble built
and rolled through him, like a
poltergeist.

In a voice all his own, he spoke,
"Strange ain't but another word for life.
Ain't a one but children and babes
what ain't carrying something.
I just ain't hiding mine."

"If you ain't got the best parts
of your daddy,
boy, you ain't got none of 'em."

Uncovering the Ashes

Cephas, age 17, finds the tin of ashes — summer

A thin-legged writing desk.
Brass chains and baroque top,
drops down like a drawbridge.
Four narrow drawers and
more coveys than he had
fingers and toes.
Old letters in blocky scrawl
filled with words.
He lets them be.

There's something fierce
taboo about a letter
that ain't yours.

Cephas still carried the pride
in his chest,
of his first piece of mail.
A bona fide correspondence
from his father's cousin in the
Eldorado penitentiary.
The hand writing went
from happy to sad
as he started out on
long last greetings and ended
reminiscing of home.
Next to the signature
stood a three-inch Garfield

sportin' six-shooters and
a bandana around his neck.

Old eyeglasses and fountain pens.
Wheat pennies.
Velvet pouch full of pumice rocks
smelling of sandalwood and church ladies.

In the back, in a shadow
an old candle stub,
a tin of powder-fine ash
tied neat with a silk-ribbon bow,
death papers and birth papers
pinned together with an
Eisenhower button.

Marl Mae sings out from the porch,

Cephas takes a wheat penny
and closes the drawbridge.

His bare feet slap down the hall.

Jon Marc Comes Home

Cephas, age 19, Lou Ellen, and Jon Marc share a fifth beneath the stars while Cephas talks — spring

"Seeing like Memphis did,
ain't what you'd think.
Most times it don't make sense.
Most times it's just feelings.
Feelings so strong and full
you'd do most anything to stop feeling them
the way you do.

"It ain't just your own,
but others' hurt.
You'd think it'd be enough to
cure a man of ever being
someone else's pain again,
but that ain't so.

"A human heart all by itself
ain't big enough to love ugly sweet.
It'll try awhile, but it'll quit.
They always do.

"Hell, a dog starts killin' chickens,
runnin' cattle,
there ain't but one cure.

"People's the same.
Turn down that road,

say, hurt themself a child.
There ain't a Savior born
of two lovers fuckin
what can untwist that sort of mind.

"Even a dog'll cower
over getting caught,
but it won't stop 'im
from shitting feathers
next time it gets loose.

"Memphis was right
to call it a blessin' and a curse
watchin' a man lose an arm
to a hay bailer, or the like.
You'll never lose one
the same way,
but neither does it mean
you'll keep yours either."

"Lou Ellen, you've
took to keepin' company
with some of the most
depressing sumbitches
a legless man
is want to know.

"I kid, Cephas. I relate. Hell,
I'd hate to see another
walk a mile in my shoes,
then again, it's not

like I'm using them.

"Honorable veteran I now am,
Cephas, I'd be honored even more
if you'd care to wipe the bottle
before passing it this way. Else,
drinking after you I might as well
take up kissing my sister."

HOPE EXISTS
The Year

Lou Ellen and the Chevy

Cephas, age 16, and Lou Ellen — winter

Since we was 14
a dozen times or better
he's run that imaginary scar
from my earlobe
to until he runs out of real estate
or the icy window knob
kisses him square on the nether.

He ain't never more handsome
than when he yelps like a pup.
Make a girl want to keep
a bowl of ice cubes around.
Just for throwing at his ass.

I knew there was something
ancient in him, even when
we was young.
So I never minded being
Maude for him.
He's the only one I never minded
tracking Mama's scar down my neck.

Men are easy to sort.
It's just hard work
finding one worth suffering for.

Cephas is angry and don't know it.

I say so cause he always gives me
his undershirt to clean up with.
Then takes it home to wash.
Being with him's like being alone
except full—
in the way of not feeling
a need for nothin'.

WHAT REMAINS
Year 4

The Machine Barn

Joela and Cephas, age 22 — winter

She smells like hospital sheets and January wind
still trapped in the fabric of a coat
before you shake it out
and hold your hands to the fire.

Dirty sunshine warbles through old pane windows.
Peels of paint and dead flies dance
on the sash in the hard winter music
seeping between glass and wood.

She doesn't stir when he rises on an elbow
to study her length.
Harsh shoulder breaking into slow curve,
butter-soft flesh,
rising hip, thigh disappearing
beneath the quilted, moving blanket.

A cooing whisper woke him.
Peering over, he sees her chin
tucked to her chest.
Hands cupped between small, hard breasts.
A flash of unearthly green
flicks beneath her wrists.
Enthralled like an outsider
witnessing an unknown ritual,
he sets a mindless hand on the bareness of her hip.
Her skin prickles against his heat and callused fingers.

The spell unbroken, she continues to whisper,
but pushes back now with her hips.

Recognizing his hand for the first time,
a sense of trespass and shame bleed into his stomach.
Yet still she pushes back against him
and the hardness between them.
Gently turning a thigh, she opens,
pressing her bareness against his flesh.
Then lust beats, beats, beats back shame.
Gut hunger drives him forward.

The whispers, never ceasing.

The faint of sweat buds along his spine.
Dew slicks between them.
He watches as the flush of warmth
spreads beneath her skin,
animating tiny hairs
backlit by the wandering sun
crawling its way over the tool bench
toward their tarnished brass bed
hunkered in the morning shadows.

HOPE EXISTS
7 Years Before

Memphis Speaks

Memphis confides the truth in Cephas, age 9 — fall

It's a hoax, boy.
If you can't see it with
two eyes, it ain't there.
Hear me, son, the water carries
only what it knows and
nothing it don't.
Blood is blood.
Leaf is leaf.
No more, no less.
All truth is God's, boy.
No truth, no water.
No water, no blood.
Just the dying like leaves,
then the fall and a cold
so lonely it burns like flames,
and the flames you step into
ain't the flames you stay
standing in.

Marl Mae was heartbroke
before she was born.
And I seen it —
coming a long ways off.

Your age, boy, maybe younger.
The truth came for me
before I knew what it was.

No one knows until
they first hear it.
Then it's clear.
Clear as light for seeing.
Like fire meant for wood,
can't nothing hide the fact
it's been touched by truth.

But hide it we will.
Try like hell.

You'll see, boy.
When the fire comes
like a hard winter,
and you got the ashes
in your hands
and nothing else
cause ashes is all you know.
You'll cry out
like a wounded bear.
Beat your chest
until all the hardness
falls away as leaves
on a dead-of-winter tree,
and all the truth
you been hiding
will be there
like mighty scars
burned deep as a coal vein
all the way to your loins,
coursed as roots

holding fast as
a valley oak
with a dam set behind
and the mountain creek rising up
to your toes and climbing
but doesn't quench.

No, son, it burns.
Like bourbon in a razor cut
steeping the truth
from your wounds
carrying some of it on
in time, in waiting
like sediment pressed
into great layers of rock
that shift when the earth
gets her hackles up
at the daring of men
trying to stop
the flow of time.

But you'll not die, boy,
nor be held forever
beneath the great sorrow.
But toil,
toil and wander you will.
Taking the truth
and carrying it in your hand
cause it's too big to fit
all at once in a broke up heart.

WHAT REMAINS
Year 4

A Chinook Wind

Lou Ellen bares her heart to Cephas, age 21, in the dying light —
winter

A chinook wind pushes Cephas
out of his coat and chambray shirt.
Sweat gathers and licks a cool path
down the back of his ear.
He hefts the maul and
lets it fall in a lazy arc.

Three times, wood heats you.
When you cut it.
When you split it.
When you burn it.

The satisfying bite and squeal
of steel cleaving wood
reverberates through sinew and bone.

Holding fast to the maul with his left,
Cephas reaches for the sledge
with his right.
Choking part way up the handle,
he steps in and windmills
the heavy hammer
in the same lazy arc.
An ear-splitting ping
sinks the maul
a solemn inch deeper.

He grunts, steps back,
steps in, and windmills again.

It's a tearing sound
like no other when
the grain separates.

Primal as a birthing groan;
ancient like atoms splitting.

Memphis always said,
hedge was the only wood
harder than a wedding dick.

Finally it gives.
The maul falls free.

Cephas takes a knee
and sets a hand to either side
of the split.
Wrenches the log apart.
The moldy piss of sap fills his nose
as the fibers still clinging
like a splintered umbilical
tear free.

One-handed, he flips the halves
onto the top of a rick.

Sweat shining golden on

his flushed chest
he takes a seat
on the chopping block
and watches Lou Ellen,
backlit by the sun,
cross the yard
with a cup of coffee
and sandwich in hand.

Full and bitter he sips
fast at the blackness, scalding his tongue
while Lou Ellen looks on.
Tearing the sandwich with his fingers,
Cephas chews slow,
studying the distant tree line.

"You love her?"

He eyes an odd shadow
waiting for it to prove itself a whitetail.
"Can't say for sure I don't."

Unmoving, Lou Ellen follows
his gaze to the tree line,
studying the blemished light herself.

Taking his coat
from its resting place,
she doubles and sets it
between his feet.

Kneeling there.

Cephas feels himself swell,
turns his face into the dying sun
and appraises the shade-covered windows on
the lee of the house.

Without preamble,
Lou Ellen unbuckles his belt
as a breeze picks up
a handful of leaves
and sends them cartwheeling,
skittering like veiny scraps of parchment
before a broom crossing a bookbinder's floor.

The shock of winter
needling the wetness of his flesh
against the plunging warmth of Lou Ellen's breath
pulls a steady groan
from Cephas like a brown bear
who knows hunger has woke him
too soon before spring.

Releasing Cephas, she rises up,
reaches for his coat and shakes it out
with a single whip.
Laying it back in its place,
she turns to the house
and walks away silent.

Groggy from half-sleep,

looking back to the tree line
the shadow is gone.

Cephas stares at the ground
between his feet, searching.

The grass, long dead, lays matted.
A scattering of bark and leaves.
An imprint of duck cloth from his coat
in a patch of dirt and clover roots
near the toe of his boot,
the only proof Lou Ellen was there.

His flesh laid sullen,
shrinking against the cold roughness
of zipper and denim
as the last of her saliva dried
in the biting winter twilight.

The Dream Returns

An augury comes to Cephas, age 21, without translation — winter

Once, no, twice
he'd seen the eyes
staring back at him
uncurious dark like the shadow
beneath cellar steps.
A fierceness, unsettling
as blood on a dove's beak.

And the dream of it feeding
at her side, burrowing like a vulture's head
between her ribs.
How she cooed and smiled
like a mother heavy with milk.
Patient, unflinching.
Then the single black feather,
a dripping oil slick
among the green.

He wakes.
Her scar beneath his hand,
still as death she sleeps
as the Quaker paces the table ledge.

Joela Meets Hope

Cephas, age 21, shares his heart with Joela — early spring

He talks. Speaks with her,
finding more to say than ever
he spoke to another. Dreams
of the house he'll build.
The future it will stand in.

He tells stories of Hope
so that she sees the girl,
senses the shallow grave of guilt
at longing for a sister
to mourn herself,
to belong somewhere
so fantastic
even death
is diminished by love.

She watches the firelight
dance and play
among the shadows
of him as he stoops naked,
working another piece
of knotted pine
into the panting coals.

Uncovering the Past

Gentry and Lomax find treasures — summer

The derelict farrowing barn squats in
head-tall horseweeds.

A tintype of itself from 1864,
after the Confederates confiscated the sum total of
Toot Van Oster's sons,
and the blue coats commandeered all but one
hog who Toot took to calling, Soul,
without which she was barren of hope.

That year Toot gave birth to her last child,
a parting gift from a Yankee trio
sent back to wait
in case Toot's rebels
were just yellowed-up and hidin' in the wood.

They blacked her eyes.
But no man's hands were as hard as
three winters' worth of war.

Fearful of ambush,
stoked by her silence,
they plumbed Rummy's great grandmother
like a well—
in wild desperation.
In the name of war and liberty.

After the coldest winter day,
the sun broke hard and strong
bringing melt to the ice,
and a slickness unkind
to pregnant women.

Soul, nosing her hip,
greedy for the honey pot in her arms,
and all else the matron had left,
sent Toot, in her man's
old hobnail boots, slipping
to all fours
in a mighty thunder,
the crock splintering
on the frozen ground.

Shit on her hands,
water streaming between her knees,
the birth pangs struck like lightning.

Too weak to rise, the first scream
came as the child crowned,
and Soul cleaved her ring finger
in haste to claim his due.

Smeared, disheveled, and bleeding,
Toot set her face to the earth in prayer,
heaving with a final mighty groan.

From beneath her overcoat and gingham dress
the bastard child tumbled

to the ground.

Blue as its fathers, the baby lay
silent as Toot.
With its face to the sky,
an ancient heathen image
of Sun god, Mother Earth bowed and
child laid beneath
its own placenta.

Finally rising to her feet,
violent stumbling carried her to the house
with her first winter tears
as she saw through the blood, her Soul
had taken her wedding band.

Fevered machetes and short handled-picks.
Kneeling, panted prayers
for double eagles and musket balls.
A shout sounds three paces
from the corner of the farrowing house
beyond the hog lot
pocked with upturned clumps
of manure and earth.

A heavyset man waddles
to a patch of carefully flattened grass
where a handkerchief lays
piled with gold-filled molars,
and sets down a dirt-caked

quart Mason jar full of rings.

Metal detector rakishly slung
against his sweat-soaked breast
like a soldier at arms.

HOPE EXISTS
7 Years Before

Fortner Takes a Drink

The night Cephas, age 9, first touched death, Fortner and Memphis
speak after Marl Mae is put away — fall

"This flesh holds a wickedness
that'll let a man eat your heart
straight from its cage
as he rocks your child
to sleep in the crook of his arm.

"You don't know what you're capable of
until the universe calls upon you
to live out your purpose.

"God Himself has revealed my end.
It comes in fire and smoke.
The idol of this body
shall burn like a crucible of gold,
and all the hearts I've ate,
and all the babies I've rocked,
and all the whiskey I've drunk,
they will all burn away.

"But the world won't be
short of wickedness,
nor the angels lacking swords.

"And the sorrow of time will rise and set
with joy and the moon.
There'll be nights of both darkness

and light. When the crows
roost early and the river runs
so black it won't carry
a dot of light. Blood will be
the only thing to ape out
the history of the stars
or catch the wink of lantern light
searching for what ain't
ready to be found."

Fortner stares long at Memphis
as silence falls behind
the old man's words.

"The wagon ride's been
a long hard road," Fortner offers
as he takes another pull
from the bottle between them.

"I seen the hurt in Marl Mae
before she was ever born.
Told her mama as much.
So it was, her mama took up
the battle unknowable
and named her Glee
to ward off the evil.
Make certain Marl always
had her own piece of joy."

"It's the wedding band
that must've split her eye.

Didn't imagine to hit her so hard.
Can't figure what part of the vows
that one fits under."

"Fortner Yoeman Purdy,
you have loved my child well.
To take a hurt into your own heart,
to ransom another's from worse,
the Word says
there's no greater love."

"Folks forget how ugly real love
can look on the surface.

"I best be off to Maude's,
to see about Hope."

Sleeping beyond the halo
cast by the porch light,
Fortner was swallowed by the night
while Cephas lay quiet,
listening through the window screen
to his father's footsteps
fade into the sloshing
bourbon bottle
tilted to the lips of Memphis.

HOPE EXISTS
The Year

Hope's Road

Fate and Fortune meet — summer

Twilight hung wounded as the squirrel-torn flesh
of a wild plum.

In places the bedrock wasn't shining clean
as worn velvet on an old theater seat,
shucks of gravel lay like sawdust on a dance floor.

Hope, pressing hard at the pedals of
Lou Ellen's hand-me-down,
leaning over the handlebars
with a reaching arm,
grabs at lightning bugs
breezing past and rising up
from the hickory, buck brush,
and wild asparagus sprouting
tall from the roadside.

The shuffle of dust and gravel
swells behind her.
Hugging the edge, Hope slows,
setting her red paint-chipped toes on the hard ground
to give a look
over her sunbaked shoulder,
before jumping clear of the bike
at the touch of something
from the bushes
wet against her stretched calf.

LOSING HOPE
The Year

Rummy Finds Another Angel

— summer

Come now darlin', Ol' Rummy will
get you where you're goin'.

Ain't you pretty as an Angel. Mama
said God made one for us all.

I'm too old to do no harm, and
it's too dark to be along here.

Snakes'll be coming out
to warm up on the road.

We'll get you where you're goin',
me and Bess will.

Ain't you a pretty thing
and ain't that a pretty ring.

Young miss, you done got me rhymin'
like a bullfrog pitching woo.

You ever eat you a frog leg?
Watch 'em kick in the skillet fat?

Get your ol' fingers slick,
lips shiny with grease.

Whitest meat you'll ever set
your teeth to. You got pretty ones

you do at that, you do.
Hey now, no need for sadness.

Ol' Rummy don't mean nothing, now.
Bess'll have us where we're headed soon.

Shhh, shhh, shhh, shhh, shhh,
you like little piggies, do you?

These here is heritage.
We won't stay long.

I just need me a few things
before I get you where

you're going.

She'll Be Okay

— summer

Shh, shh, shh, hey now,
Puppy, she'll be okay.
It's all okay.

A picket fence of tree trunks
stutter past the headlights
stretching the edges of the darkness.

Cur dog whines and worries
the still warm body
under nose and paw,
drawing life to the surface
in the scratch of her claws.

The truck shudders and stumbles
across ruts, and rocks too big
to move from the trail.

Snot and tears stick
to the whiskers
of the alien face
in the dash light.

A shiver crawls and lightning
strikes his mind
ushering more bleary-eyed drops
every time the fingers

of a dying branch
reach out for a fender,
gouging their epitaph
in the dust and paint.

Lord I'm sorry, Mama.
I ain't no good,
no matter my tryin'.

Jon Marc and the Corporal

Jon Marc deploys — fall

"The education of a man doth not begin
until he has drawn first blood.
Be it with manhood or mortar,
God will be called upon in either event,
or you're not doing it right.
In which case I'd rather face
an enemy wounded than an angry woman.

"The poets, the romantics, sages and sergeants,
they all have it wrong.
Love and war are one in the same,
and whiskey is the Switzerland of the heart.
Declining sides, it finds itself surrounded
when it's just here to have a good time."

"I knew your family was farmer types.
Just didn't know they raised bullshit."

"We've sand in our cracks and chinks in our armor.
Dust in our eyes, and Hajis a-storming.
So pick up your SAWs and lay down some cover,
while ol' Jon Marc here switches out rubbers."

"Boy, you is ate up as anyone I seen.
A pig's had more Muslim pussy than you.
The only territory you conquering
is a hole in the sand."

"You wound me, young Corporal, wound me deep.
To have so little faith is to make me wish for
Cephas Purdy. My brother, my rock. He would be
first to explain the foundation of my theory
civility calls for becoming one with the land
before landing one for cumming in.
And where is this pig?
It would seem he has a few pointers to offer,
if not lunch."

God Damns It All

Fortner struggles as the anniversary looms — summer

The neon paints a mortician's glow
on the face of every patron.
Christmas lights dangle merry
from the antlered whitetails
bursting through the walls.

Fortner takes a stool,
tips an abandoned glass,
emptying the contents before
the barkeep takes it away and wipes clean the oaken bar,
setting a draft and coaster in its stead.

Twang and sorrow pine through the jukebox,
through the mad frenzy of billiards
escaping an early morning break.

Fortner Yeoman slides the mug aside,
raps a tawny knuckle on the hardwood,
not bothering to catch the barkeep's eye
until a tumbler of bourbon
finds its way to his lips.

Shakes of tobacco crumble between
his calloused fingers tucking
the corners of a rolling paper
like a blanket at his child's shoulders.

A cacophony grouses its way
loutishly into Fortner's ear.

"Everybody ain't in love
with the sound of your voice
so shut your goddamn soup-cooler
and mind your goddamn beer."
Ham-fisted Charlie, the barkeep,
extoling the virtues of
shut-the-fuck-upness
the unslept, stiff-necked,
late-morning besotted sometimes
blaspheme in ignorance.

"What kind of goddamn person
lets their kids roam along
the road at night?"

"I tell you now
and tell you true,
Milo Bittle,
you'll be gargling teeth
like a shit salesman
with a mouthful of samples
if anything but rotted breath
and cigarette smoke
escape your gin hole again."

A glorious vein
blunting the bisecting furrow
of Fortner's weather-beaten brow

grows with every heartbeat,

as a pure ribbon of red

finds its way from Fortner's nose,

hesitating then breaking from his lip

in a drip

to gather upon Milo's face

like a ketchup smear

at the corner of his mouth.

Fortner Yeoman Purdy's speed

carried away all logic but breathing

and the bladder's function

from Milo's mind where he lay

prone as a tit-weary kitten

across the neighboring stool.

Fortner's hand at rest

around Milo's neck

felt sanctified as a marriage bed

and final as a burial suit,

until Reverend Charlie

blessed the union and broke the spell

with the gentle nudge of his Louisville slugger

against Fortner's wild chest.

"Purdy, you know Milo's

no better suited to sense

than squattin' to piss.

Now take this napkin here,

you're bleeding some."

The sudden fire of daylight
coursing through the side door
blanched the darkness,
leaving Fortner's negative
burned into the eyes
watching him depart.

Fortner Hears the Lights

Fate calls on Fortner as he leaves the Neon Sign — summer

He holds a hand out before his face
against the blaring, late morning sun.

The petrified bones of old mountains
crunch beneath his feet.

The slam of his truck door brings
his mind to its knees.

Insulated from the world, the familiar
smell of dirt and rust floats

among dust motes rising from the seat
to settle on the dash.

Gravel spins beneath his tires.
The angry grunt of metal

reverberates through the stick shift,
jarring the marrow of his arm.

The old truck smokes and howls
its way onto the pavement,

Milo's words carry him through
the stop sign.

A great rumble of thunder bursts,
releasing a rain.

Pierces his skin.
Washing him, washing him

in tumbling madness
like a polished rock.

The sunlight screams
a low siren's wail

glaring off the glass-soaked pavement.
The Hunter's constellation

melting into the macadam
tattoos his corneas

as he gazes across the brilliant chaos
of blood and glass and shit.

Screaming. Relentless. Drills
into what's left of Fortner's ear.

Voices and squeals, and
a sideways walking pig,

draws Purdy to his feet
where he rises and rises

as a newborn mountain growing

with every shiver and birth pang

the earth beneath ushers from parted lips.
Bodies and steel litter the road.

Before him a mighty boar laps and tugs
at the hairy rind of a scalp laid bare.

A savage kick to the animal's face
spirits another grunting squeal toward the ether.

The scalp twitches and Fortner finds
a pleading eye whining as a child,

"Bury me with my angels. Bury me
with the bones of my angels."

He spills forth bile and whiskey,
sadness, and fear of Milo's words.

LOSING HOPE
Year 1

This House of Fire and Ash

Memphis' words again come to pass — summer

Every shade of sunset and danger
slapped and pulled each other in escape,
crowding up the length of creosote-
choked stove pipe,
glowing cherry at the roof line.

Acrid black smoke
belched up from an attic
steamer chest draped in a yellowed, white-lace gown
as the house took a sighing breath.

Blackening, flagellate cancer
lapped at the fireplace mantle
like a dog with blood on his muzzle.
Shadows of tongues danced
across the walls and
hovered like a crown
atop the head of Memphis
like the day of Pentecost
as he slumbered in whiskey stupor,
drawing his fill of smoke.
While the voice spoke,
Memphis panted and danced
in the roaring of the dream.

The Roaring of the Dream

Memphis dreams as the fire burns — summer

And the Mobius scrolled,
and the words came
as Thunder beckoned, "SPEAK, MAN, as a tree.
Speak, anointed by fire and heaven.
Prophesy the above.
Speak like blackened toenails at the stake,
as scorched root
nursing at water's edge."

And Memphis parted his lips to speak,
and from them poured coal
and ash and water and time.

 . . . and the village burned.
The children screamed like stark heat.
Their safety lay silent in pools of death and excrement.
Even the dogs which came
to feed lay slain,
so that silence covered them
but for the flames
and screams of children
until the fire filled their eyes
with violent whipping and slashing,
dancing until the burning tongues consumed
their wailing,
their tears,
until sorrow became void of expression.

What do the young know of sorrow?
 All they have lost they have not earned.

Out of the fire and screaming,
out of the stark heat I was born.
The slayer of dogs who come to feast.
I am the whipping and slashing,
the violent dancing,
the absence of unearned sorrow.

I am counted among them,
though cannot tell you their number,
cannot tell you their names.

Some became soldiers, mercenaries
of ferocity recited
by the score and fatness of the dogs who followed them.

Some became millers,
circling and grinding, circling
and grinding
as though the stones were tethered about their necks

Some became whores.
The wisest and most beautiful found
following only the fattest dogs

Some became wild,
living among the briars of summer,
the stones in winter,

until season upon season crushed them
as with the miller's wheel.
By feat of will the hungriest alone
survived by hunting the fattest dogs.

So it was. The sons of soldiers,
and sons of the wild were born together—
all were counted as sons.
In seasons spare of flesh and fire,
the sons of millers
were sown and born among them as well.

Shelters rose and millraces were dug
to screams giving way to the cries of children.
For in the crying there was light,
and no son was distinguished from another.
And the dogs were sated by the afterbirth,
the people upon bread and fancy.

Then the sun set on the ripest day.
The millraces ran with blood,
grinding the flour of rage,
and a great wind carried it as a plague.

Restlessness became brooding fear,
and with it the darkness.

Desiring light, torches were lit,
and the light revealed the sons had divided.

The dogs began to pant,

and the village burned.

The children screamed like stark heat . . .

HOPE GONE
Year 2

Marl Mae Gathers Her Daddy

A year to the day Marl loses hope — summer

Nubbed and charred by the fire,
the redbud nearest the house
held a scattering of still green leaves
at its outstretched fingertips,
as a mother holds her child
free of harm's reach.

The fire marshal swore Memphis
must have made his bed
on a pallet of rocket fuel,
to have burned so hot.

Foundation stone crumbled under
the weight of her foot
like a desiccated fairy ring.
Careful to step in the boot prints
laid out before her,
Marl Mae felt the melt of
powder-fine snow harden
against the heat of her
bare feet forming a wild
paw print within each track.
Stretching and hopping to match
her daddy's stride across
the snow-covered field to
a giant oak, twice anointed by heaven.

She finds the bed rail with her toe,
watches the blood pool in the
spilt of nail and flesh.
The powder disappearing at its edge
like melting snow flakes.
Sits down amidst her daddy's ashes.
Foot in hand, Marl studies the blood,
washing a wandering course
the length of her sole, as it
leaves a mercy red jag of lightning
tattooed through the dirt on her skin,
striking in drops as it falls from
her heel and bursts
on the ground, splattering puffs of still warm ash.

A modern Job, she falls
to her back in the powder-fine ash
and sweeps her limbs like a child
on a blanket of snow.

A bridge to the ether,
Marl Mae turns to lay
hands to hands,
feet to feet, and
face to face,
setting her lips to the ash angel.
She screams primordial brokenness,
wrenching every bit of life
from her lungs.
Patiently waiting
to feel the rum-tum

of her father's heart
rise from the ground.

As the sun sets and the night cools,
she licks the ash from her lips
and rises to her knees.
Making a reliquary of her hands,
Marl gathers ashes
from the chest of her angel
and wanders into the night.

Witching the Passing Gate

Rummy's burial — summer

Rummy sat bundled in his own meat locker
a week until word could be got to his sister,
and came back the reply:
SO BURY HIM - - Stop.

The heritage hogs sold at auction
to pay for the box and service.
Where an old-timey neighbor,
for the sake of Rummy's long-gone mama,
put pennies on his eyes
and two twigs of alder
in the pocket of his shirt
to well-witch the Passing Gate
in case his sins had went unconfessed.

From a shoebox beneath her arm,
to undo the undertaker's work,
she pulled a clod from the first
shovel of dirt turned to dig his grave
and raked it across his heavy palms,
dragging his fingers one by one
through the blood soil of his people.

As a man liveth, so he is to die.
He digs his grave by the work of his hands,
and a farmer without dirt beneath his nails
won't fit in any grave for long.

Nolo Contendere

Fortner pleads no contest — fall

Fortner stood before the court,
grizzled and worn.

The bus, long and grey, windows barred,
wobbled through the potholes,
bucking as it pulled from the gravel.
Northbound across the iron bridge,
leaving the two-lane leading home.

Towering walls swallowed them,
a stone dragon with dead men for teeth.

Deloused and pale as the moon, in used boxer shorts
that waggled his manhood through the fly,
like firewood, Fortner carried his
bedding, boots and clothes
from one dead man to the next.

"Lift your shaft, open your mouth, squat and cough."

"Grab your punks and press your bunks.
Mind your own so I don't have to mind it for you.
You got a complaint? Take it up with the judge.
I'm here to feed you, count you, and bury you—
if breathing gets to be too much.
Enjoy your stay."

Twelve hundred souls flowed as a single, pacing lion.

Marl Mae Goes to Church

Marl Mae says her piece before God — fall

Antebellum cap-and-ball revolver swinging free,
her finest sunhat and toenails colored pink,
Marl curtsied to the good Reverend,
the cross, then sacraments.
With flourish, she turned to doff her bonnet,
tapping the barrel to her brim.

From a clenched fist,
a worthy part of her father
in powder-fine ash
amidst a crumpled wad of bills
dropped into the offering basket.

Taking up the Blood like a brandy glass
and settling her china-white ass
on the organist's velvet stool,
Marl downed the Savior in a mouthful,
slapping the chalice, with a clatter,
to the floor.

"I'm no Virgin Mary, but I got an ass
all the same, to propel me
wherever the hell I wanna go,
and it's raw for all the noses
busy judging it.

"So here you have it laid bare.

Get a damn good look before it's gone
cause the next batch of casserole-toting
gossip-whores knocking at my door
will know the fury of hell before
their quim clear the bottom step."

Unrushed as a Sunday breeze,
Marl ran a hand between her thighs
and shushed the lips off
Reverend Good's most devoted sheep
as she passed by the front row,
strolling out the way she came.

The Sheriff Intercedes

The Sheriff speaks with Cephas, age 17, about Marl Mae's commit-
ment — summer

Sorry about this, Cephas.

There ain't nothing for it,

but them Docs'll help

get her cheese

back on its cracker.

What with Fortner going up

there ain't nothing for it, son.

Memphis, your grandmother,

one of them's always been round

to keep an eye, get her back right.

Son, you got to know this ain't the first

. . . Sweat lines in his uniform

paint sickly dark smiles

beneath the sheriff's tits . . .

It's been a hard few years,

what with losing Hope,

your granddad passing.

It'd be hard on any woman.

. . . Fortner made religion of

never trusting a man

with an ass wider than

his shoulders . . .

. . . The sheriff's words blur into the tick
of the box fan pulling late summer
through the cluttered office . . .

Boy, it's hotter than two rats fuckin'
in an old lady's sock drawer.
Can I get you a Coke?

The Writing Desk

Cephas, age 17, retrieves the ashes — fall

Fingering the chiseled top,
the dust nesting
in baroque crevices.
Skin and earth,
polished past.

The drawbridge,
coffee tin, candle stub
Eisenhower button campaigning
constituents in death.

Cephas takes up generations
light as Bible pages.
Certificates of births and deaths
draw the salty sweat from his hands
as blood to the lips of ancients.

Memphis would have laughed
to know himself
billeted by Hills Bros.'

The voice of Lou Ellen
sifts through the screen door.

He leaves the drawbridge down
and a wheat penny for the toll.

Maude Takes Cephas In

Cephas, age 17, with Fortner upstate and Marl committed — fall

Just until you're eighteen, Cephas.
The house and the barn ain't going nowhere.

Jon Marc will be leaving soon for school.
Having you will make missing him
into something a little less.

She pulls him close to hug.
He rests his chin
in the cup of her neck.

Sweat and perfume fill his nose
as Lou Ellen traces a finger
around his ear.

Two Winters Pass

Jon Marc rehabs at Walter Reed — spring

Even if I give you three swings,
you know this still ends with
me pissing in your butt.

"That's a son-of-a-bitch
thing to say."

Well life's just
a string of son-of-a-bitches,
Nubs. If you ain't figured it out
by now, you never will.
Fate gave you two good arms.
Apparently you squandered
the use of them, so
she took 'em back.

As for me, I'm a rambling man.
Out of the environ of war
I have evolved like
the finches of Darwin.
Tell me wheels are not
a more efficient means
of mobility and travel.
Take note of my future progeny.
Beneath the microscope,
this very day you'll find
the gametes waiting

at the starting gate,
bolstered for speed by
little tiny training wheels.
Just like their dear old pa.

Matter-of-factly,
my well-promised GI bill,
and subsequent royalty check
for the privilege of fertilizing
the desert with my extremities
will go solely to research.
An in-depth study.
Starting with a control group
of these fat-bottomed nurses,
ending with whatever
I drunkenly wake up to.

WHAT REMAINS
Year 5

SUMMER

Cephas Dreams of Ashes

The Gift weighs heavy on Cephas' mind

A gray sky and muted screaming
like a rifle shot in heavy snow.
He trips and stumbles over sticks and bones,

falls to his face,
face to stone, like egg shells breaking.
Eye to eye with shattered bone.

Takes it up in hand
to peer through the socket,
see from where it sees
where the blood ran,
the fire danced
in tongues
he sees and hears the singing
sweet in the fire dance
the wood and stone
Trips and stumbles over sticks and bones.
Sweet the singing, can't be screaming
as he looks the world through ancient eyes
of fire and bone
and tongues speaking
ancient burning
singing sweetly, maybe screaming
he trips and stumbles over sticks and bone

Hoot at the Asylum

Marl Mae talks with her friends

Green grass green, have you ever seen
so green a grass.
Shed some blood and you'd never know
it wasn't Christmas
if not for the lack of reindeer
and bells on bobtails ringing
that's lovely red hair see
how it goes with the green
we might not have to shed
any blood after all
says Hoot which is me
and that's why I say it.

Marl Mae offers a starry-eyed stare
to the sky and laughs
along with the first drops of rain
as Hoot wiggles the toes
in his argyle sock kept safely
tied around his neck.

They're not really toes you know
but they used to be.

Marl grins at the thought of knowing
toes,
pulls a handful of grass free
by the root

just to hear Hoot scream.

Don't you think he has a lovely
screaming voice, Isaiah?
      The orderlies come but never
          in order.

Smell the earth with me, Isaiah. It will be
"Delicious," I'm told by the dirt eater over there.
Full of this and that extinct.

Perhaps we'll become dinosaurs
before the orderlies arrive to take us
away from the rain.

                Everything good gets taken.
             That's history straightening up
                before the future arrives.

That's why there's no such thing
as looking forward in fondness.

                  Marl, I do wish you
             wouldn't make him scream.

How can you know you're alive
if the pain of living doesn't cost you anything?

Then dinosaurs we'll be.
Living as unknown toes in a sock
around a crazy person's neck.

Says you, Marl.

I can feel the heartbeat of the earth
and it sings like an angel.

Joela Finds Work

Cold, chrome bed rails laugh back
at the fluorescent lights.

"Hey, little darlin',
you my new bedpan queen?"
the wispy voice rattles
like a muffled string of squibs.

"Watch out for that one.
Eyes don't work, and
neither do his willy,
but his hands is fine."

"I can hear you, ya know.
Let me at the Doc's ear.
I'll be chasing you round and
round with a little blue pill."

"Pete, don't
no one wanna do
the house-slipper shuffle with you,
ya crusty old bastard.
Leave this girl be."

"If you're so set on being rid of me,
try being nice to lil' Old Pete.
Might give me a hard attack
and you somethin' to smile 'bout."

Treasure Hunters at the Neon Sign

Gentry and Lomax peddle their wares

The jar shines polished
as a genie's lamp worn
to the last of its wishes.
Like clattering six-pennies,
rings belch from its mouth
as Gentry shakes it over the bar—

bands of gold and tin with stones of every color,
a dozen delicate crosses set with tiny Saviors.

"Rich. Boys, this here's
what a little hard work will do for you."

"Work's sure enough something
your fat ass knows little about."

"Jon Marc, mean
for mean's sake,
ain't for heaven's sake."

"Gentry, take your God, you little words
your pile of trinkets, and go
eat a shit sandwich. Kindly,
I suggest take it off the bread
so as not to foul the taste.
This bar was sweet heaven,
until your sweat-soured ass

ambled in to sully it
with talk of work and deities other
than amber liquids of carbonation and fire.
You got any thoughts on politics too,
or is there nothing here left sacred?"

Jon Marc ponders the rings,
a tousled pile of lives.

"If you ain't robbed a pawn shop
there's a cemetery somewhere
with a case of the pox.

"Where you all been?"

"Nowheres near a graveyard,
I'll tell you that."

Cold, silent, Cephas sits dumb,
staring at a silver mood ring
before taking it up.

"You like that one, Cephas?"

"Where you all been?"

"Out to the woods
looking for musket balls and sabers,"

"You got to three—"

"Three what?"

The blood pours from Gentry's nose,
bows to the floor in cursing prayer.
Cephas turns Gentry's first pain
into a mercy with the swing of a beer mug
and growling scream, "You tell me how
you found my sister's ring."

Cephas Travels to His Father, with the Ring

Yeoman loses Hope

"Before they bury me, son,
Have 'em bind my hands and feet.
Else, do it yourself.
When it's time for dying
I ain't going peaceably,
and I want it known
eons from now, if ever dug up,
I fought to the last drop.
You take a man's hope and the Cosmos'll
avenge it so he pays double.
Seems that's just drama for drama's sake.
A man's pain ain't for amusement,
but you couldn't tell it from these walls.
This sky and the shadows cast.
The Greeks were a sick people to believe
in so many gods when just the one's
cruel enough for all his wisdom."

"Yeoman, a couple of fellas
was treasure hunting the Van Oster place
and pulled a mason jar of rings
from the ground. Tell me
this here ain't Hope's."

"Doing so won't take old whiskey from my breath.
They find any bones for the sheriff to sort?
Hers will sing you know, like warm vinyl

in the marrow. You was born with
the bigness of the sky in yours.
Hers were born with music.
It's something, cause your mama's voice
will defeather a song bird."

"The sheriff says a dime store ring
don't mean nothing. And there was plenty
others with diamonds and gold."

"Tie my hands and feet, son.
Bind 'em fast, for all the more
say I had in this life."

Jug Lining

Joela and Cephas fish on the river

The brown river runs
slow through the oaks.
A cigarette hangs from his lip.

She sits
small in the bow
studying his face
wishing
she were the smoke
kissing his cheek.

Sun dappled fish scum
atop the wind-scaled water.

An old bleach bottle jogs,
dips its neck,
like a feeding mallard
flashing its moon-white ass
in wild Morse code.

Cephas grins at her
childlike delight,
perching near the edge
waiting,
the Quaker on her shoulder.
His own little pirate queen.

The motor cuts to a burbling shudder,
pisses
a tiny rainbow slick in death.

Out of the newborn silence
the zizz of braided nylon
rubs against the oarlock
as he pulls
hand over hand
the thousand-pound cord fighting
its rise to the surface.

Muddy water flecks sinuous arms,
drips from his fist.
He reaches
bare handed
into the cold,
grabbing thunder,
heaves until it
claps and rumbles
in the tail of a catfish
wrestling against
the bottom of the jon boat.

Hope Laid to Rest

Cephas hopes to heal Marl Mae with closure

I hear her hum.
Do you hear her hum?
In the evenings
when the crickets start to cry
and the nightjars call,
my, oh my, she sings.

"We're going to put a date
on the stone, Mama,
the same as when they found her ring."

That rock ain't marking nothing
but the mulley grubs, you know.
Hope ain't beneath that stone.

Do you ever hear her singing?
You should hear her sing.
She carries time like the river.
Takes you right on down with every word,
my sweet girl.

"They ain't found all the bones.
Though most was in the hog yard,
there's testing yet to do."

Stay until the blood meridian
sets that lightning tree on fire.

You hear her sing, and you'll see
she ain't beneath that stone.

FALL

Jon Marc Confesses the War

Jon Marc finally shares his burdens with Cephas

There's a bitterness to it
like a burning mattress.
Oily bitter, with a sweetness
that almost reminds you
of the 4th of July.

Until you realize the bitterness
is burning tires and diesel,
and the sweetness of July
is burning PFC, Holder
— that's "Boulder Holder" to you —
and your mouth waters
from the smell and urge to vomit.
And you think of his blistered
snow-white bitch-tits
from his first week in country,
and his mother's chocolate chip cookies.

I'll tell you about philosophy,
the rights of men,
purpose and destination,
civility contracts and governments —
by the people, of the people
for the consumption of people.

It's all about socks.
You'll never understand how important

socks are, until you go to war.

I'd give my legs to go back
to thinking about socks
like I did when I was nine.

The Wedding

Jon Marc officiates the union of Cephas and Joela at the Neon Sign

You're certain you're certain?

Love is about contact between soles.
Ten up and ten down in a row.
Before this cloud of witnesses,
do ye rightly confess to have curled each other's toes?

I'll take her blushing
and your witless grin
as admission of guilt.
Does anyone within the sound of my voice
find fault with this here union
of girl and boy in howling mattress-moaning?

Ergo, I, hereby
the pull-out method and
the seat of my pants,
through the power invested
by Jack Daniels, the United States Army,
Chaucer, Josey Wales and Twain,
pronounce you,
Hand and Knife.

Wield each other carefully
as you carve each other's hearts
out in the world round about.

Here's where I'd tell you
to kiss the bride
if I didn't fear your lips
will be worn out before
you get to my ass.

Be gone, be well, be generous
with the KY and bug repellent.
Apply both liberally, avoiding
contact with eyes and mouth.
if swelling persists after two weeks
discontinue use and call your physician.
Like this,
"Barkeep Charlie, a round
for the cappy houple's parson.
And them too!"

Joela, Cephas, and Jon Marc at Somersby's Grocery

Picking up supplies for Cephas' 22nd birthday

Cephas kicks at a rust stain
beneath the wax of the polished floor.
The musty smell of boxed produce.
Sterile cans of corn and butterbeans
sad succotash
under cold fluorescents.

Rattling warble of shopping carts.

"You reckon it's funny how the baskets
look like cages?
Even after it's shot,
cooked and canned,
bagged and wrapped,
seems we're still afraid
dinner's gonna get up and make a run for it."

She giggles at the thought,
studying a boxcar of animal crackers
before adding them to the basket
in Jon Marc's lap,
as he takes up the thread.

"Hunter-gatherers. Certifiable.
Clear through to the subconscious.
We clubbed, first women, then seals.
Then our dented women convinced us,

'Give up thy sacred clubs to
crib everything from babies to corn.'
Cephas, I must agree."

"I say Joela's subject to dent your head
and use it for a serving bowl
if your mind wasn't so shallow."

"All I ask is potato salad, please.
Or better yet, swing
a dozen times and make it deviled eggs.
To be bludgeoned by this hospice angel
smacks of salvation and pleasure.
If heaven's the party they say,
how could St. Pete refuse
a serving platter on wheels?"

The Vows

Cephas speaks his heart to Joela on a trip to the mountains

Although I know the pleasure
of embracing discomfort.
How a man comes to feeling out of place inside,
how he grows to find home in the hardships
offered up by nature,
how pain becomes a familiar friend,
bearing the truth he is alive,
how it makes the soft things richer
when he grants himself permission.

Like the feel of clean, dry socks
pulled over cold, wet feet,
the bristle of heat on wind-chapped skin,
the smell of clean sheets,
the touch of a woman.
How flesh warms against flesh.

How beneath the fumbling coldness of winter
you can sense the warm flow of blood
coursing like a thousand tiny rivers
eroding away the cold, flake by snowflake.

Even after sky beats earth, it seems.
Where a truce is drawn
below the blanket of white.
The drifts rising higher than a horse and man.
Where, like God with the oceans and tides

saying, "You shall come this far, but no farther."
the earth and the blood strike accord with cold.

Where whiteness and stillness win out
until flesh touches flesh and doesn't flinch away,
and in the touch, blood senses blood,
and the discomfort and hardness become
unbearable for their sameness,
and the cold melts.

Where fear and listlessness come together,
where softness and hardness are confused,
and sight bends, where sky and earth meet,
and the horizon can't be trusted,
I'll cling to you until faith gives in
or the mountainside appears.

Milo Bittle Toasts the Couple and Eats His Teeth

Milo provokes Cephas

"Careful there, girly.
The Purdys ain't exactly
tightly wrapped,
and something ugly seems set
on dogging their people.

"I'd light-out while
the day's got some sunshine left.
Less of course you ain't drinking
on account of a bastard seed.
Ain't too late
to find a banker's son.
Let him nut in you.
Pass that baby off as respectable."

A tessellated explosion of teeth and blood
sounds off at the muted rifle-crack
a pool cue makes when laid
clean across a grown man's jaw.

Cephas throws a stony glare
at Milo's slumped visage,
as Charlie dials the law.

Hugging the Quaker to her chest
while Cephas cleans the spray from
her cheek, Joela wells with tears.

Joela Cozak

Joela uncovers her past

An old courthouse of ancient stone—
second growth pinewood floors creak beneath
the weight of her steps,
seasoned by a thousand footfalls
carrying generations.
Lemon oil and judgment
stagnate the air
like a hospital that's lost its power to heal.

Slope-shouldered, hugging
the little green bird to her chest,
she stops short of the stairs
leading to the basement cell
where Cephas passes the days.

A postcard of etched tin hangs
framed in cherry wood on the wall.
The Quaker stirs at her breast.
Edging closer to the photo,
Joela looks into the face
of her flint-eyed and sober mother
with a rugged brood of Confederate-dressed men
flanking the steps of a deep, log cabin porch.

"Van Oster Farm"
April 23, 1865

Joela's ribs begin
to separate,
smells the sudden sharpness
of blood pouring
from the web of her thumb
in the parrot's beak.

Easing her grip, it shudders,
sliding free to the floor.

A revenant stagger
carries her to the door.
Leaving blood on the glass,
Joela stumbles out
and is swallowed by light.

Cephas Takes to the Woods

Cephas jumps bail and goes on walkabout

A hard freeze holds loneliness
in the air like falling ash.
Ham-fisted Charlie waits in Cephas' truck.

Gravel crunches beneath his feet like old bones
beneath the gristmill of eons.

"You the one?"

"She just asked me to bring your truck."

"Tell Jon Marc I went feral."

The machine barn is empty.
Their bed, cold.

Cephas waits for the darkening of the sky.
Sets no fire in the stove.
Shivers and waits.

Gathering his pack and pole,
he lights out for the pines
of the deep wood.

Cutting trail straight up the sides,
he rises with the moon and falls
a little less each time,

foraging light to walk by
from the night sky greeting
everything willing to let it shine in.

A full night and day, he tracks
a ragged path until the blood rose of dusk
blooms on the last ridge.

Cephas stops to suck the sweat
from the shoulder of his shirt.
As the meridian fades dusty red,

music calls sweet to his marrow,
drawing him like the hope of
water and time.

And so he walks, and the music
is overrun by tears and moans
leading him to a sullen form.

Stretched across a pile of stones
swollen and disfigured, he finds
Milo Bittle crying a mother's tears.

Milo Remembers

A blurry thump.
Dead weight against steel
brings Milo skidding to a halt.

Propping himself up
against the truck, he makes a
slow inspection around the front
finding nothing
but the passenger mirror
folded and spidered.

Looking for the beast in the ditch,
he stumbles hard and lands soft
with his face on a cushion of
belly flesh and Dollar Store perfume.

He lays quiet against the flower,
unable to remember the last time
something so soft, smelling
so sweet, touched his face.

The driving spike of a whimper
pierces the fog
behind his eyes.

Pushing up, he looks at the form
sprawled before his bowed knees
between the twisted legs.

The ruby wash of taillight
shines like oil in the
wetness of her eye.

Again the whimper.
Fear and hope shower sparks
in the blackness of his mind.

The weight of his hand
lolls her head to the side.

Another whimper rises
as a dog,
now nosing the muss of tangled hair.

Walleyed, Milo throws himself back,
scrabbling on bloody palms and kicking heels
from the shadow dog and the sweet softness.

Milo Hears Her Sing

Milo makes his peace

You can hear her, can't you?
Singing sweet as she lay in the ditch.
I didn't mean for it to be so.

Have you ever heard something so lovely?
My heart can't take it, for the way she lays here.

She ain't alone. Never alone.
I took her dog, and buried it too.
Let no blood. Just took its breath.

She never stops, you know?
Singing.
Twice, I've built this mound.
Taken her deeper, farther still.
Still she sings. She sings,

and boils in my heart
the black of my wickedness,
my awful self.

I bring her flowers,
and sleep sometimes
here among the stones.
I plead with her,
though I have no right.

Death won't come for me.
Lord, I've tried, but I fear it.
Fear it so.

See these flowers here.
You won't forgive, though.
You won't, you won't, you won't.

Don't let it be bloody, no.
Could you do that for old Milo?

If you can't forgive,
just don't let it be bloody.

Cephas Finds Hope

And loses a little more of himself

At the pile of turned stones
At the dirt beneath his finger nails
At the dying fetor of his sister
At the sunlight dappling her bones
At the singing now ceased
At the rush of creek filling the silence
At Milo Bittle as the sun rises and sets
At the blush of old-world crocus
Blooming at his temple
Where the blood pools darkly
Beneath the skin,
Cephas sits and stares.

WINTER

Cephas Visits Marl Mae, She Tells of His Sins

Cephas' world continues to unspool

You grow like no weed I've ever seen.
Sweet Cephas, has it really been three years?
I told you she sings. You heard her I know,
beneath the stones where you buried Milo.
Bittle makes her smile, and he cries no more.
You did right to seek the river and listen.
I see you're holding St. Helen's ashes.
But you must know them ain't Memphis, dear.
I scattered him to the mountains and river,
baked him into the crust of a dozen pies,
fed him to them gawkers hawking judgment.
That tin of dust you got there, sweet Cephas,
is the hot tears of a raging mountain.

The Raven Leads Him

Cephas searches for something to hold on to

He travels the gravel roads,
driving slowly
to where the vows spoke.

The wrinkled groan and iron rip
of his truck door punctuates
the quiet until a raven caws,
flying from the top of the
lightning pine.
Following its path
through the gray winter trees
moaning with the wind,
he hears Joela, knows
she's found her way,
where flesh meets the numbing cold
and flesh touches flesh,
and in the touch, blood senses blood.

Smells the smoke of burning logs.
Trudges further, towards the warmth.
He finds her blurred
by the heat of fire, feet
splayed in the snow
as a man he doesn't know
takes her flesh in his,
and the raven flies,
and the groaning grows,

swelling deep
as the cold white rising
higher than man and horse.

Lou Ellen there waiting, waiting
for his shadow to fall away,
a whitetail melting into the trees.

Cephas Goes to Maude

Hungry and desperate

Beneath the hangman's bulb,
in the heat of her kitchen,
Maude holds Cephas among the tears
staining her chest,
and coos to him the things of men.

Until the warmth of lips painting
the scar at her neck are not pursed
in forming words,
but speak breakingly to her heart.

The scar growing darker still,
"The night you near drowned
in the river with Marl,
your daddy kissed me there."

St. Helen Erupts Again

Revenants show themselves in the dying light of the day

He finds the dog, with gouged-out eye,
whining as it worms along,
emerging from the trees,

stumbling, starving, from the field,
and knows it. Knows it to be,
in the milk-white orb of blue.

Swings a wild kick and misses.
Falls weeping to his knees,
sorrowful for the meanness of it all.

Takes the blind cur in his arms
holds her trembling
against the fear and the cold.

The wind blows and whistles
through the old Ford's cab,
washing a leaf around in circles

tumbling, tumbling, tumbling.
Cephas takes the Hills Bros. tin,
prying free the lid,

ash whirls up faint as a ghost
as he holds the can in hand,
holds it out the window

burling like a coal-fired steam engine,
scattering dust like dying smoke
along the highway.

Near Where the Blood Pools

Cephas gnaws on the root of bitterness as he talks to God

It's a cold hill, this mountain and its snow.
A dark maw like the caw of a blackbird
winging about as a pristine flake
with a mind of its own.
One flies and somebody dies.
Two and it's just a thing to see.
More than that you have yourself a murder.
All these omens for naught.

They don't stop the blue from coming,
just trick you into being scared for it,
like a banker that keeps charging interest
even after she sees the foreclosure coming
wrapped up with a bow.

There ain't nothing for it.
This goddamn hill, this cold
mountain and its snow.
Came too soon and stayed too long.
Her and her eyes.
And the scar
beneath her left breast
and ruddy nipple.
Where my lips rested
like she was something real.

That murder of crows.

Then the one flying off.
I should have known.
Who wears a black dress with roses
to their own wedding?

This dirty snow,
blue like milk and the thin violet
of a dead man's cheek
right near where the blood pools.

You can see it farther off now.
A big ugly maw
like a crow's caw echoing off
this piss-ugly mountain.
With its stark whiteness
and its dead-man's skin,
and them two blackbirds.
That should have been an omen of some kind.
With her and her knifepoint scar
she said came with her childhood.
Though she couldn't remember how,
except for the murder of crows
and that cold goddam hill.

Acknowledgements

I owe a debt of gratitude to far more people than I've listed here, but to name a few: Dr. Jon Marc Taylor, who believed so strongly in the healing power of education he invested not only his money but his life to the cause of rehabilitating men broken like he once was. Jon, you may have died in prison but you didn't die alone. I'll see you again on the other side.

Fitz and Michelle, thanks for everything — your friendship, your resources, your hard work and constant encouragement, and especially for all those stupid greeting cards that make me laugh and remind me to keep loving others.

Chris Helvey, you're a good egg my friend, and one of my favorite story tellers. Thanks for your guidance, and giving me that first shot in *Trajectory*.

Fred Chappell, your friendship, gentle guidance, shared wisdom and wonderful writing came at a time when I needed them the most, and have forever broadened the path of possibility.

To my first readers: Fitz, Michelle, Mike Porter, Chris H. and Pete, thanks for jumping on the grenade.

To my Editors and company: Joe Taylor and Eleanor Boudreau, you're my kind of writers, and your patience has been otherworldly. Thanks for everything.

To all my girls: Virginia Terry, my favorite person in the world, who with her life showed me how to love others. I'm sorry I was such a slow learner. Mama T. and mama Deb, where would I be without a couple of old broads like you? Thanks for putting up with my crap long after I was out of diapers. Sandy and Kate, home will always be with you. Jamie, you're the real deal, and you deserve the world. Audrey, Adelynn and Nevaeh, two of you are not allowed to read this book for at least the next 20 years. Buefort, thanks for keeping me laughing, and answering the question "If you really knew me, could you really love me?"

Finally, from one poetry bum to others, Stewmeat and Skullface, I'd have expired on the tracks without you guys.

Last but not least: Landon Prothro, for helping me keep hope alive; Lake Watson, one day my brother, one day; and finally, Jensen, welcome to the world. Be brave, little man.

Author Photo: Dennis Powell

About the Author

After taking another man's life under questionable circumstances, Ben Terry has spent the last two decades incarcerated in his home state of Missouri where he's serving a sentence of Life Without Parole. Currently he divides his time between training service dogs and rescues; working in production at the prison's closed circuit TV station; and writing. His poems, short stories, and essays have appeared in several different journals including: *Trajectory, Rattle, Coal City Review, The ReSentencing Journal,* and the *Tulip Tree Review. Near Where the Blood Pools* is his first book.